HOW TO BE AN EFFECTIVE PARTICIPANT IN SPECIAL EDUCATION TEAM MEETINGS

HOW TO BE AN EFFECTIVE PARTICIPANT IN SPECIAL EDUCATION TEAM MEETINGS

A GUIDE FOR PARENTS

Ways for Parents to Actively Partner with Staff in SPED Team Meetings

Robert Scobie, MA, PhD
Founder of Common Goal, LLC

*Tell me, I may listen.
Teach me, I may remember.
Involve me, I will do it.*
– CHINESE PROVERB

White River Press • Amherst, Massachusetts

How to Be an Effective Participant in Special Education Team Meetings: A Guide for Parents

Copyright 2014 by Robert Scobie, MA, PhD
All rights reserved.

Book and cover design:
Douglas Lufkin, Lufkin Graphic Designs

Other than the form templates for personal use, no portion of this book may be reproduced or used in any form, or by any means, without prior written permission of the publisher.

White River Press
P.O. Box 3561
Amherst, MA 01004
www.whiteriverpress.com

ISBN: 978-1-887043-10-6

Library of Congress Cataloging-in-Publication Data

Scobie, Robert, 1936-
    How to be an effective participant in special education team meetings : a guide for parents / by Robert Scobie, PhD., Founder of Common Goal, LLC.
    pages cm
    ISBN 978-1-887043-10-6 (pbk. : alk. paper)
1. Special education--Parent participation. 2. Parent-teacher relationships. I. Title.
LC3969.S356 2014
371.9--dc23
                        2014005425

TABLE OF CONTENTS

Introduction.. 1

Part One: Preparing for the Team Meeting................ 5
   Step 1: Make Sure Your Goals Correspond to the Team's
      Objectives... 5
   Step 2: Work with the Case Manager to Develop an Agenda . 7
      Worksheet: Develop an Agenda....................... 8
   Step 3: Build on Your Child's Strengths 10
      Worksheet: Child's Strengths 11
   What are Your Concerns? 13
      Worksheet: Parents' Concerns 16
   Force Field Steps 18
      Worksheet: Force Field Description & Analysis...... 19

Part Two: Participating in the Team Meeting............ 21
   Check List of Key Points 21
   Discussion Strategies 22
   Problem Solving 22
   Freeing Responses 22
   Ask Questions 24
   Know your Hot Buttons 24

Part Three: Meeting Closing and Follow-up.............. 25
   Meeting Closing 25
   Meeting Follow-up 26

Conclusion 27

Resources 29

HOW TO BE AN EFFECTIVE PARTICIPANT IN SPECIAL EDUCATION TEAM MEETINGS

INTRODUCTION

During my 15 years as a special educator in elementary and secondary public schools, I witnessed the value of having the parents of special needs children become actively involved in their child's education. They have:

- shared personal information that helped the staff know their child better;
- acted as important advocates for change if things were not going well for their child;
- supported and encouraged their child while he or she worked at home on school assignments.

We know that when educators and parents work together to support learning, the children benefit. They achieve better results in school, stay in school longer, and like school better.

Though federal special education (SPED) regulations require parents to be involved with their child's education, the complexities of the SPED process often make parents uncertain about how to get actively involved; parents often question the value of their input. But because school team members and parents have different experiences and knowledge about the child, if they share their perspectives in constructive ways, they can help the child reach his or her potential and avoid misunderstandings throughout the process. Because neither federal nor state regulations provide guidance for parents as to how to prepare, participate, and follow-up on meetings, this guide has been created.

Imagine yourself, a parent of a special needs child, getting ready to participate in a school team meeting to develop your child's evaluation plan, to review his or her evaluation results, to plan his or her Individual Education Plan (IEP), or to problem-solve a behavior issue. You know that these tasks deal with technical issues of learning, issues that the school staff are more familiar with than you are. But you are your child's advocate. You, as parents, know the characteristics, strengths, and weaknesses of your child better than anyone else. Your ongoing relationship provides you with a wide-angle view of your child. Because the school staff members are professional educators, they often only see your child through the lens of their particular area of expertise.

You might be eager to participate, but you might worry that your involvement can ultimately have negative results. For example:

- you might feel intimidated to face professional educators in the meeting;

- you might worry the staff will blame you for your child's difficulties in school and you might, in turn, become defensive;

- you know you've had problems with your child at home, but you might be skeptical about staff's willingness to listen to your concerns. If they discount what you say with, "Yes, but..." how will you respond?

This guide is intended to provide you with guidelines and encouragement to help you participate effectively in the SPED process and, especially, in the team meeting. It is organized into three parts:

1. Preparation for the meeting

2. Participation in the meeting

3. Follow-up to the meeting

Follow the guidelines and use the checklists. And remember that you are an important member of your child's special education team.

PART ONE:
PREPARING FOR THE TEAM MEETING

By taking a few specific steps, you will be better prepared for the team meeting. Steps include:

- Identify your concerns and goals for the meeting.
- Meet with your child's Case Manager to discuss your concerns and goals, and to fill out an agenda form.
- Identify your child's strengths and interests.
- Respond to a checklist of questions about your child's academic and behavioral problems.

STEP 1:
MAKE SURE YOUR GOALS CORRESPOND TO THE TEAM'S OBJECTIVES

In preparation for any team meeting, it's important for you to be clear about your goals and concerns for your child. Communicating these to the team will help ensure that your goals correspond with those of the school staff so you will all be working toward the same results.

Though regulations require parents to be involved in the SPED process, if you feel anxious or skeptical about being on the team, this might hinder the effectiveness of your participation. To offset this, remember that two-way communication based on trust and openness is important. But as shown in the parent's story below, two-way communication is not always easy to achieve.

> **A PARENT'S STORY**
>
> When my son, Ben, entered school I noticed that he was having difficulty learning to read. I tried to get help from the school system, but they just put him in special education classes. I knew that there were other options that might help Ben that the school system wasn't trying. I went to my husband to try to explain. I knew what I wanted to say, but I couldn't relay my feelings in a way that he could understand. I went to the school system to try to explain, but because I couldn't speak education jargon, I couldn't get my point across to them either.
>
> – *The Diary of a Family with Dyslexia,* by Dorothy Tod

To help the team function effectively, two-way communication is vital. For you, as parents and team members, the important question is: how can you ensure that the school staff listen to, understand, and respect your concerns about your child?

A good starting point is for you and the Case Manager to meet before the team meeting, preferably in your home, for an in-depth discussion about your concerns and your participation in the upcoming team meeting. Both you and your child's Case Manager should fill out an agenda, which will include the following:

STEP 2:
WORK WITH THE CASE MANAGER TO DEVELOP AN AGENDA

Please refer to the templates on the next two pages when creating your agenda.

- **ITEM:** Write a title for each item or topic that needs to be considered. Use one line (or box) per item.
- **DESIRED OUTCOME:** Insert the result you would like to have for each topic. This is perhaps the most important step in agenda planning.
- **PRIORITY:** Identify high-priority items. Rank the items in order, noting that those not covered in the meeting can be addressed at the next meeting.
- **TIME:** Projecting the time you need is easier if you've planned the "how" and "desired outcome" parts of the item.
- **WHO:** This is the person who will be responsible for seeing the item through to completion.
- **HOW:** This relates to the process for dealing with the item. Do team members need to engage in a dialogue or a discussion? Do they need to brainstorm alternatives or reach a consensus? Should they be given feedback? Etc.
- **TASK COMPLETED:** After the person responsible for each topic has addressed and completed the task, insert the staff's initials and date here for future reference.

Make a photocopy of the blank template on the next page and fill it out prior to each team meeting. Completing the form validates your goals and gives you a clear voice in deciding how they can be achieved. (If you enlarge it by 122% while photocopying, the form will fill an 8.5 x 11 sheet.)

ITEM	DESIRED OUTCOME	PRIORITY	TIME	WHO	HOW	TASK COMPLETED

An example of a completed agenda filled in by parents and their child's Case Manager follows. As you can see, the parents' and the Case Manager's concerns were focused on the child's behavior and writing skills.

ITEM	DESIRED OUTCOME	PRIORITY	TIME	WHO	HOW	TASK COMPLETED
Tom's behavior	Identify probs./success	High	15 mins.	Case Mgr.	Dialogue/Discuss	
Behavior plan	Change-address problems	High	15 mins.	Behav. Spec.	Present./Discuss	
Writing problems	Identify difficulties	High	10 mins.	Case Mgr.	Present./Discuss	
Writing progress	Modify to motivate Tom	High	10 mins.	Teacher	Discussion	

STEP 3:
BUILD ON YOUR CHILD'S STRENGTHS

As you prepare for the team meeting, think about what you know about your child. Whether his or her problems are academic, social, and/or behavioral, you are aware of them. But, make sure you focus on the positives as well. The school staff will want to build on these assets while working to improve your child's disability.

Make a photocopy of the form on the opposite page, then use it as a checklist to identify your child's strengths. This will enable the school staff to provide successful experiences.

_____'S STRENGTHS

Check the appropriate boxes of statements that match your child's capabilities:

☐ Follows-through and completes tasks.

☐ Copes with changes in routine.

☐ Problem-solves when obstacles arise while working on a task and engaged in an activity.

☐ Copes with transitions like changing activities, stopping an existing activity, getting up in the morning.

☐ Completes homework and turns it in on time.

☐ Keeps track of time and schedules.

☐ Keeps track of possessions (books, notebooks, etc.).

☐ Manages frustration when unable to complete a task.

☐ Plans ahead or thinks before acting or speaking.

☐ Tries out new things; takes risks.

☐ Acknowledges and accepts individual differences.

☐ Acts independently.

☐ Shows enthusiasm about things of interest (music, art, mechanics, electronics, pet care, etc.).

☐ Shows awareness of his or her strengths and weaknesses.

☐ Helps with household tasks.

☐ Plays cooperatively with other children.

☐ Adapts to new social situations.

☐ Shows understanding of how his or her behavior affects others.

☐ Communicates his or her preferences and/or needs.

☐ Accepts responsibility for his or her behavior.

☐ Engages in physical activities with other children, such as playing catch, tag, kicking a ball, etc.

A PARENT'S STORY

"I think Devon has Attention Deficit Hyperactivity Disorder," the kindergarten teacher whispered in my ear. I paused with no reaction. It sounded like my son had just been diagnosed with some terrible, incurable disease. The blank look on my face must have somehow urged her to continue on.

I knew Devon was difficult, I even read the book, "How to Raise a Difficult Child." I loved my son. Nothing was wrong with him. I began my quest to prove it, mostly for myself and especially for him.

– *ADHD – One Mother's Perspective*, by Kathleen Turner

A child's attributes should be presented as strengths not as weaknesses or disorders. "Easily distracted," "short attention span," "disorganized," "impulsive behavior" – all can be viewed in positive ways such as: "constantly monitoring the environment," "the ability to switch tasks on a split second's notice," "very independent," "thinking for oneself," "flexible," "incredible bursts of energy," "thinking visually," "will face danger that others will not," "a willingness to take risks," and "quick decision making."

A PARENT'S STORY

At nine, John was already four to five years behind in reading. His teachers said he was inattentive and disruptive. We were totally unaware that he was dyslexic until one of his teachers explained, almost in passing, that this pattern of behavior was relatively common in dyslexic children. His doctor stressed that this was a life-long problem, and we would need to develop long-term strategies to build on John's strengths in order compensate for his weaknesses. John was a particularly good swimmer but, we asked ourselves, would the time he was spending swimming be better spent on extra work for school? At the end of the day, we decided that his most important need was to feel good about himself. He needed some shield against the "stupid" taunts he was getting from other children.

– *Dyslexia to Dreams – A Parent's Story*, by Raymond Gibbons

WHAT ARE YOUR CONCERNS?

In ancient mythology, it was believed that calling an evil spirit by its name would enable you to ward it off. So, too, with problematic behaviors – identify them and you break the spell they cast: your focus for problem solving is out in the open for everyone to see and to deal with directly.

A PARENT'S STORY

Ribble, the school counselor, pulled out old standardized test scores for Louie, going all the way back, that showed wild inconsistencies. He said the tests and Louie's school record suggested my son was not only "visually processing impaired" (Henrico County's official term for dyslexia), but that he likely had attention-deficit disorder, and was suffering. Ribble pointed out this possibility again and again, mostly because I denied it firmly every time he said it. "I'd know if he was struggling that much," I protested. "I'd be able to tell." But I hadn't. I had ignored the clues because I didn't want to see them. Besides not being able to read much, Louie was habitually disorganized, couldn't absorb instructions that went on for very long, and was easily distracted by sound or movement. All signs of ADD.

When I told Louie about the diagnosis, he didn't look hurt or confused. Instead, his face relaxed and he shouted, "You mean I'm not stupid?"

I was so taken aback that I started to cry.

Louie said, still very relieved, "Were you worried, too?"

I cried harder.

– My Son's Disability, and My Own Inability to See It,
by Martha Randolph Carr

It is vital for you, as parents, to recognize how important you are in helping school staff identify and understand any problem(s) your child is having. Your relationship with your child provides you with intimate knowledge of him or her. Keep close track of your observations of your child. Be descriptive of his or her behavior.

To help you get started, make a photocopy of the questionnaire on the following page, then write your responses on a separate sheet of paper to share with your child's Case Manager.

PARENTS' CONCERNS ABOUT _____

- What are the behaviors about which I'm most concerned?

- How long have I noticed them?

- What seems to trigger the misbehavior?

- What difficulties does my child have in reading, in solving math problems, or in other academic subjects?

- How difficult is it for my child to complete his or her homework?

- What works to get him or her to complete the homework or to control his or her behavior? What doesn't work?

- How does my child feel about him- or herself?

- How does he or she express feelings when happy? Angry? Sad?

- What does my child like to do? What doesn't my child like to do?

- How does he or she get along with other kids? with adults?

- What do I think the problem is?

You might suggest that the Case Manager use the problem-solving strategy called Force Field Description & Analysis. This strategy is very helpful in identifying the underlying causes of your child's performance and behavior in school and at home.

The example below depicts a description of a fictional fourth grade student's (Tom Bruno) Force Field. To prepare one for your child, photocopy the blank template on the following page and fill it out, using the example below as a guideline. Share it with your child's Case Manager.

EXAMPLE FOR TOM'S FORCE FIELD DESCRIPTION

Goal(s)

Tom needs to:
1) *increase his self-management skills in order to control his aggressive and disruptive behavior;*
2) *work more constructively with others in a group;*
3) *sustain attention to the task during desk work;*
4) *show increased motivation to write about topics of interest.*

Current Situation

FORCES FOR	FORCES AGAINST
Pro-Social/Academic Behaviors & Contexts	Problem Behaviors & Contexts
1. Wants adult approval	1. Peer rejection
2. Seeks out one-on-one time with teacher	2. One close friend; distracting
3. Offers help to other students	3. Isolates self from group
4. Avoids conflict if not his issue	4. Needs teacher more than other students
5. Likes National Geographic books; likes to read	5. Follower
6. Can write in complete sentences	6. Problems when given choices
	7. Can't do independent desk work
	8. During group instruction, Tom doesn't understand directions for independent work
	9. Dislikes writing; no motivation; lacks skills

FORCE FIELD STEPS:

1. In the column under **FORCES FOR**, list the behaviors and contexts that enhance the student's movement toward the goal(s).

2. Under **FORCES AGAINST**, list behaviors and contexts which block the student from achieving the goal(s).

3. To analyze the Force Fields (e.g., behaviors and contexts), ask the following questions:

    - How clear are you about the behavior and contexts as a force?

    - How important is the behavior as a force? (E.g., the most important behavior is one that, if changed, would yield the greatest movement toward the goal.)

    - How easily can the behavior and contexts be changed?

4. Based on the Force Field Description & Analysis, develop an action plan for the student.

FORCE FIELD DESCRIPTION & ANALYSIS

Goal(s)

Current Situation

FORCES FOR

Pro-Social/Academic
Behaviors & Contexts

FORCES AGAINST

Problem Behaviors
& Contexts

PART TWO: PARTICIPATING IN THE TEAM MEETING

Before you go into the meeting, make a list of the following key points and bring it with you. During the meeting, feel free to refer to the list in order to be sure the agenda is productive and responsive to your needs.

CHECK LIST OF KEY POINTS:

- Ensure that the school staff is respectful and responsive to your concerns;
- Check to see that your goals correspond to the team's objectives;
- Share your observations about your child to help identify the problems;
- Share information about your child's strengths and interests;
- Prepare to use discussion strategies to enhance your participation and advance toward your goals (see examples below);
- Review relevant documents;
- Clarify the communication process.

When you enter the meeting room, greet the staff in a friendly and confident manner. The Case Manager will begin by presenting the agenda. Make sure your concerns and goals for the meeting are clear to the staff.

DISCUSSION STRATEGIES

During the meeting, be aware of whether you feel accepted as a member of the team. Ask yourself: "Is the team addressing the questions/concerns that are important to us?" "If not, how do I redirect the discussion?" Be prepared to use the following discussion strategies:

PROBLEM SOLVING:

- View the team as partners in problem solving. Jointly decide the nature of the problem(s) to be addressed.

- Share your own observations and ask for concrete information from the staff. A clear definition of the problem with supporting evidence is imperative. One helpful strategy for problem solving is the Force Field Description & Analysis. Ask your Case Manager to share your work on this with the team.

FREEING RESPONSES:

To enhance openness, review the list and practice those behaviors you would be most comfortable using in the meeting.

- Listen attentively; paraphrase to understand, not simply to repeat what the other has said. If you want someone to listen to you, begin by listening to him or her. If you want someone to acknowledge your point, acknowledge the other's first.

> *"Let me check out what I understood you to say."*

- Check impressions of the other's feelings.

  > *"I hear some frustration behind your statement."*

- Seek information to understand the other.

  > *"In order for me to understand your view, I need more information."*

- Offer information that is relevant to the other's concern.

  > *"I'd like to add some information to what you've already given me."*

- Describe observable behaviors that influence him or her.

  > *"It seems that you're very accepting when someone argues with you."*

- Directly report your own thoughts and feelings and provide specifics to help the school staff picture what you are thinking and seeing.

  > *"I feel frustrated by your opinion regarding..."*

- Offer your opinions or state your value position in an open way.

  > *"I think we can make the process more efficient."*

ASK QUESTIONS:

- **ASK WHY.** Treat another's viewpoint or position as an opportunity rather than an obstacle.

- **ASK WHY NOT.** If another is reluctant to share his or her interests, propose an option and ask: "Why not do it this way?" or "What would be wrong with this approach?"

- **ASK FOR THE STAFF'S ADVICE.** For example, say, "What would you suggest that we do?"

KNOW YOUR HOT BUTTONS:

- To calm yourself, pay attention not only to what the other person is doing, but also to what you are thinking and feeling.

- If you encounter negative behaviors, don't take them personally.

- If you feel "attacked," it may help to see the other person as someone who doesn't know any better.

- Directly report how another's behavior makes you feel.

PART THREE: MEETING CLOSING AND FOLLOW-UP

MEETING CLOSING

Before the meeting closes be sure to:

- **REQUEST A SUMMARY** of the meeting minutes in writing with a list of any decisions that were made, so that you are clear about the decisions agreed upon and the next steps to take.

- **ASK FOR RELEVANT FORMS THAT REQUIRE YOUR SIGNATURE.** Parental consent is required for any of the following:

    - Conducting an initial evaluation;
    - Providing initial special education and related services to a child with a disability;
    - Annual renewal of the IEP and placement of a child with a disability;
    - Determining or changing the disability classification;
    - Changing the nature or extent of the special education and related services;
    - Conducting a re-evaluation.

    Check to make sure that what you are being asked to sign agrees with the decisions made during the meeting. If you approve, sign the appropriate form(s). If you disapprove, take the form(s) and document(s) home and study them further.

- **REQUEST WAYS TO COMMUNICATE.** Ask about the best way (e-mail, phone, written) and time of day to communicate with the Case Manager and/or the classroom teacher.

- **REQUEST TRACKING INFORMATION.** Ask about the best way to keep track of the implementation of team decisions.

MEETING FOLLOW-UP

Meeting follow-up is equally important. Be sure to:

- Make a follow-up call to the Case Manager to discuss the meeting. If you had taken any relevant documents home for further study, suggest changes you think are necessary and decide what the next steps should be.

- Share your reactions – both negative and positive – with the Case Manager to your being part of the meeting. This is likely to be helpful in regard to future meetings.

- Tell the Case Manager how often you want to be informed about how your child is doing.

CONCLUSION

As a parent of a child with special needs, you have a responsibility to work with his or her Special Education Team. By learning to participate in a successful SPED team meeting, your meetings will be more productive and satisfying to all parties. Your child may be part of his or her school system for years to come, so take the time to study this book and use the tools. Your child – and you – will improve the process and benefit from the results.

A companion guide to this book has been written especially for Case Managers. *How To Create Successful Special Education Team Meetings: A Guide for Case Managers – Techniques for Engaging Staff and Parents to Make your SPED Meetings Productive and Positive.* It is available at Amazon.com, Barnes & Noble, or at www.effectiveSPEDmeetings.com.

If you would like information on how to arrange for a meeting with Robert Scobie, contact him at bob@effectiveSPEDmeetings.com, or visit his website at www.effectiveSPEDmeetings.com.

RESOURCES

Among the references below, the author wishes to acknowledge his indebtedness to the following for their strategy ideas: Richard A. Schmuck, Philip J. Runkel, William Ury, and the Pacer Center.

Barrett, Jon H., *Individual Goals and Organizational Objectives*, Ann Arbor, MI: Institute for Social Research, The University of Michigan, 1970, 3, 11.

Fisher, Roger and Ury, William, *Getting to YES*, (MA: Houghton Mifflin Co., 1981.

Schmuck, Richard A. & Runkel, Philip J., *Handbook of Organization Development in Schools*, University of Oregon, Center for the Advanced Study of Educational Administration, National Press Books, 1972, p. 233.

Schmuck, Richard A., Runkel, Philip J, Arends, Jane H., Arends, Richard I., *The Second Handbook of Organization Development in Schools*, CA: Mayfield Publishing Co., 1977, pp. 91-92.

Tableman, Betty, "Parent Involvement in Schools," *BEST Practice Briefs*, No. 30-R, (June, 2004), University Outreach & Engagement at Michigan State University, Lansing, MI.

Ury, William, *Getting Past No: Negotiating with Difficult People*, NY: Bantam Books, 1991.

WEBSITES:

web.mit.edu/hr/oed/learn/teams/index.html
How and Why to Use a Meeting Agenda

www.ldonline.org/firstperson
Personal stories from the world's leading website on learning disabilities and ADHD.

www.rti4success.org/resource/parent-page-what-responsiveness-intervention
NRCLD is the National Research Center on Learning Disabilities. The website contains research on RtI (Response to Instruction and Intervention) and Office of Special Education Programs (OSEP) information.

www.pacer.org
PACER (Parent Advocacy Coalition for Educational Rights) represents the PACER CENTER ACTION Information sheets. PACER Center is a parent training and information center for families of children and youth with all disabilities from birth through 21 years old.

www.pacer.org/parent/php/PHP-c156.pdf
Parents Can Prepare for Special Education Meetings

www.pacer.org/parent/php/PHP-c144.pdf
Planning for a meeting about your child's behavior needs

www.pacer.org/parent/php/PHP-c136.pdf
Use Questions to Find Answers: A guide for parents of children receiving special education services

www.pacer.org/parent/php/PHP-c96.pdf
Parent Keys to Success In the Parent-School Partnership

www.pacer.org/parent/php/PHP-c82.pdf
Communication in the Special Education Process

www.pacer.org/parent/php/PHP-c186.pdf
A Place to Start: Understanding the Present Level of Academic Achievement and Functional Performance Statement

My thanks to the following for critically reviewing earlier drafts of both books and providing thoughtful suggestions: Craig Barringer, Phil Eller, Lyn Haas, Nina McCampbell, Windham Northeast Special Education Compliance Improvement Team, & Joanne Scobie.

I also thank Jean Stone for editing my manuscript, Douglas Lufkin of Lufkin Graphic Designs for making it look great, and Linda Roghaar of White River Press for publishing my books.

The information contained herein follows federal guidelines for special education. Please refer to your individual state to be certain all information is correct for and appropriate to your state.